You Loved

Yes you are loved Diane,
I love you very much
Irlene

by
Alma Kern

Illustrated by Martha Werner

Acknowledgments

Scripture quotations (marked TEV) are from TODAY'S ENGLISH VERSION of the Bible. Copyright © American Bible Society 1966, 1971, 1976.

Biblical references marked RSV are from the Revised Standard Version of the Bible, copyrighted 1946, 1952 © 1971, 1973. Used by permission.

Quotations marked KJV are from the King James or Authorized Version of the Bible.

Verses marked TLB are taken from THE LIVING BIBLE © 1971. Used by permission of Tyndale House Publishers, Inc., Wheaton, IL 60189. All rights reserved.

Unless otherwise noted, the Scripture quotations in this publication are from The Holy Bible: NEW INTERNATIONAL VERSION, 1973, 1978, 1984 by the International Bible Society. Used by permission of Zondervan Bible Publishers.

Library of Congress Cataloging in Publication Data
ISBN 0-9614955-1-0

Special thanks
to my husband
for his patient love,
his sound advice.

He helps me believe
I am loved.

Dear Readers,

"I pray that Christ will make his home in your hearts through faith. I pray that you may have your roots and foundation in love, so that you, together with all God's people, may have the power to understand
  how broad
   and long,
    how high
     and deep,
is Christ's love. Yes, may you come to know his love—although it can never be fully known — and so be completely filled with the very nature of God."
      (Ephesians 3:17-19 TEV)

TABLE OF CONTENTS

You Are Loved

God loves you
> though you feel unloved or unlovable.

God loves you
> with a love that is undeserved and unchanging.

God loves you
> as you strive to please Him;

God loves you
> as you insist on doing your own thing.

God loves you
> during times you praise and thank Him;

God loves you
> during times you ignore and doubt Him.

God loves you
> if you are content with the pattern of life;

God loves you
> if life makes no sense, seems unfair, unjust.

God loves you
> when you are surrounded by family and friends;

God loves you
> when you are lonely, rejected, heartbroken.

God loves you
> while you are healthy and strong;

God loves you
> while you are sick and weak.

God loves you
> if you are happy and successful;

God loves you
> if you are miserable and discouraged.

God loves you
> whether you are glad, sad, mad or bad.

God loves you
> because God is love.

Everybody Is Somebody

We tend to love those we find lovable—
people who give us what we want or need,
persons with whom we share a point of view,
those who are grateful and kind,
or whose helplessness is appealing to us,
or who are like us.

Our Lord demands: love your neighbor.
Who is our neighbor? Everyone who needs our love.
We cannot pick and choose whom we will love.
Nor can we love only when we feel like it,
or just when we are loved in return.

It's hard to love certain people.
How can we love the undeserving, the unworthy?
Only as we accept and appreciate God's love
can it flow through us to other lives.
It takes the Holy Spirit's power in us
and a lot of discipline on our part.

*"God has poured out his love
into our hearts by the Holy Spirit. . . .
God demonstrates his own love for us in this:
While we were still sinners,
Christ died for us."* (Romans 5:5b, 8)

Though we are undeserving and unworthy,
our Lord loves us!
Still we ignore Him, disobey Him.
God hates our sin but loves us sinners.
Because He loves us, He takes our sin seriously.
Because He loves us, He sacrificed His only Son.

Each of us can be sure of this:
God loves me just as I am.
His love forgives, heals, restores.
It can transform me.
With God's love working in me
I can love myself and my neighbor.

I am a beloved child of God.
My neighbor is also a beloved child of God.
Our Father means for the two of us
to love each other.

I see my neighbor in a new dimension.
Everybody is somebody—
deeply loved by God, made in His image,
purchased at great cost by Jesus' blood.

Often people do not act like God's children.
They live as lost, unhappy, homeless orphans.
Yet my Father insists I love them.
I may not be fond of them,
but I must work for their highest welfare,
overcome evil with good, pray on their behalf.

God loves those around me through me.
I am the delivery system for His love!

Love God

"Love the Lord your God
with all your heart, with all your soul,
and with all your strength." (Deuteronomy 6:5 TEV)

That's not a suggestion.
It's a command!
It's the law. The royal law!

We do not naturally respond to God's love with love.
So He insists on it—
not only for His glory but also for our own good.

How do we love God?
"This is love for God: to obey his commands."
(1 John 5:3a)

Love must be freely given.
But we have a will of our own
that has always gotten us into trouble—deep trouble.

When Eve was tempted in the Garden of Eden,
she didn't want to be like Satan.
She wanted to be like God,
but foolishly she disobeyed His command.
Adam didn't need much coaxing to do likewise.
The relationship with the Creator was broken!
Adam was afraid and tried to hide from the Lord.

Sometimes our failures loom so big we try to hide from God.
But too often we get so used to sin
we hardly know that it is sin.
It's difficult for us to make sincere confession
if we don't even remember specific sins.

We know God has given us the Ten Commandments.
Yet we often act as if God isn't looking,
that He doesn't really mean what He says, or that
He winks an eye and permissively lets us do our thing.

When we confess and repent, God forgives for Jesus' sake.
We must not take His forgiving love lightly.
We must not reason: "God likes to forgive.
I like to sin. What a combination!"

It is so easy for us to obtain forgiveness
because it cost God so much.
He paid an awesome price!

*"For God so loved the world that he
gave his one and only Son. . . ."* (John 3:16)

*"We all, like sheep, have gone astray,
each of us has turned to his own way; and the
Lord has laid on him the iniquity of us all."*
(Isaiah 53:6)

Holy, precious Jesus took the rap for our sin!
How much He loves us! What amazing grace!

As we grow in appreciation of Jesus' enormous sacrifice,
we will put more effort into obeying God's commands.
Because He first loved us, we will strive to
love the Lord with all our heart,
with all our soul
and with all our strength.

This Is Love

" Dear friends, let us love one another, for love comes from God. This is how God showed his love among us: He sent his one and only Son into the world that we might live through him. This is love: not that we loved God, but that he loved us and sent his Son as an atoning sacrifice for our sins. Dear friends, since God so loved us, we also ought to love one another. No one has ever seen God; but if we love each other, God lives in us and his love is made complete in us."

(1 John 4:7, 9-1

Love Yourself

When you look in a mirror, don't just say, "Ugh!"
If you talk to yourself, say an encouraging word.
Tell yourself, "I love you. Just as you are."
Cheer yourself on. Be positive.
Recognize your potential for improvement!

The King of the universe is your heavenly Father.
You may not look like a princess or prince—but you are.
You might not act like one—but you are.
Sometimes you don't feel important—but you are.

Though you fail to love Him, others and yourself,
your heavenly Father goes on loving you.
Your sin is despicable, but you are of great value.
God's only Son was sacrificed on your behalf.
If you believe Jesus died for you, God forgives you.

The Lord says to you, *"You are precious in my eyes,
and honored, and I love you. . . . "* (Isaiah 43:4a RSV)
You honor Him when you prize what He treasures.
Respect yourself and you glorify your Maker.
He expects great things of you.

God loves you. Love yourself.

How to Love Jesus

"I was hungry and
you gave me something to eat,
I was thirsty and
you gave me something to drink,
I was a stranger and
you invited me in.
I needed clothes and
you clothed me,
I was sick and
you looked after me,
I was in prison and
you came to visit me." (Matthew 25:35-36)

Jesus
gives us
tasks that are down to earth,
which, after all, is where we live.

Not
colossal challenges
but ordinary human things
can give evidence that we love Him.

Great
occasions to serve our Lord
come very, very seldom.
Little ones surround us.

Forgive Yourself

O Lord,
how could I be so dumb! Dumb! Dumb!
I showed up for a doctor's appointment the wrong day.

The results are not earthshaking or tragic.
I can retrace my steps and do the whole thing over.
But I was humiliated and disgusted!
And it's frustrating to think of time and money
wasted because of my carelessness.

It's hard for me to forgive myself.
I don't like being a failure,
failing at such a simple thing.
Yet the more I concentrate on squandered opportunity,
the harder it is to pull myself together.

Thank You, Lord, for being willing to forgive—
not only sins I commit, but also mistakes I make.
You don't think I'm a failure.
Enable me to forgive myself. Help me remember:
	Though I fail,
	I'm not a failure.
Give me a clear mind and the skill to undo
what I can and make amends where necessary.

Thank You for my loved ones who comfort me
saying, "Anyone could have made that mistake."

May I remember the pain I feel today—
not to pound myself into the ground,
but to be more understanding of others
who make mistakes, even stupid ones.
They need my patient, encouraging love.

God Is Love

People can know God's power by
observing it in the natural world.
We may recognize God's wrath by
perceiving it in the events of history.
But we come to know God's love
only as it is revealed in His Word.

The Old Testament tells how
the Lord rescued His people from enslavement.
The Exodus was God's great act of deliverance,
evidence of His redeeming, faithful love.

God gave His chosen people a set of laws
to remind them they were special.
*"If you obey me fully . . . then out of all nations you
will be my treasured possession."* (Exodus 19:5)
They were slow to learn.

The Israelites were not grateful just to be
the object of God's affection and attention.
They expected to be a privileged people
with the Almighty as their willing servant.
They wanted to be pampered and protected.
He wanted them to be faithful and courageous.
They wearied Him with their grumbling and complaining,
angered Him by their disobedience and rebellion.

Patiently the Lord used the testings of
their wilderness experience to shape them up.
Before they reached the Promised Land,
they had to learn to trust Him to guide and provide.
Only then could they go forward with the confidence
that with Him nothing would be impossible.

The New Testament tells of God's greater rescue plan.
To save us from eternal slavery to Satan,
God sent His own Son to deliver us.
God took our nature.
Jesus became one of us!
He went about doing good.
He always did what pleased the Father.
But He was rejected and crucified.
Jesus' death was more than an execution.
It was a sacrifice!
He died in our place.
If we believe in Jesus, we shall be saved—
made fit to enter the Promised Land!

Life here on earth is our wilderness journey.
It is not perfect—never will be.
There will be frustration and weariness,
testings and trials.
Our desire is to be pampered children.
The Lord wants us to be faithful and strong.

We ought not doubt our Father's love and wisdom
every time something goes wrong:
"How come God does this? Why doesn't He do that?"
Instead we must learn to ask:
"Lord, what are You trying to teach me?
How can I honor You with my response to this trouble?"

We have the assurance:
" . . . the Lord surrounds his people
both now and forevermore." (Psalm 125:2b)
"The eternal God is your refuge, and
underneath are the everlasting arms."
(Deuteronomy 33:27)
"God is love." (1 John 4:8b)

Tell the Love of Jesus

Lord,
You want me to tell others about Your love?
My faith is too personal to discuss with others.
I'd feel foolish. I don't like to be rejected.
You expect more of me than I care to do!

I prefer to do mission work in other ways.
Think of all the hours I volunteer at church—
making things for the bazaar, serving at suppers.
The money goes for missions to demonstrate our love.

But I just can't talk about my faith in You.
I don't know what to say. Frankly, I'm scared.
I guess You could say I suffer "back trouble"—
there's a yellow streak running right down it.

O Jesus, You know what it is to be scared!
In Gethsemane You sweat great drops like blood.
At Calvary You faced more than rejection.
You willingly suffered agony of body and soul.

You did this for me because You love me!
Since I believe this, I'll be with You forever!
You died for everybody in the whole world!
Some of my friends and neighbors don't know it.

I must not clasp You selfishly to myself.
You were the Father's message of hope.
Now You send me to be Your messenger to others.
My life must illustrate the good news I bring.

You don't expect more of me than You empower me to do.
Lord, I'm available. I promise to be Your witness.
Put someone in my path today with ears willing to hear.
Fill me with Your Spirit so I speak the truth in love.

Loving Service

Lord,

Often
I serve
because it is my duty.

Sometimes
I serve
because it enriches my life.

Never
must I be more
devoted to service than to You.

You love me
not because I'm useful to You.

You love me
because I am precious to You.

Help
me serve
only in response to Your love.

Love Begins at Home

We learn to love by being loved.
Love makes people feel they are worthwhile.
It's the most important experience in life.

Do I love my family? They are my nearest neighbors.
Except for a spouse we do not select our family.
God places them in our care. He wants us to love them.

Do I let each one know: you are a special person?
By word and deed I build up or destroy self-esteem.
We live in a harsh world. At home we need to be loved.

Do I promote family harmony?
Each has different schedules, standards, goals.
All need to be encouraged, reassured, reinforced.

Are people more important to me than things?
Earning money, buying goods and taking care of them
must not absorb all my time, thought, energy, devotion.

Am I concerned about my family's spiritual well-being?
It is my privilege to share with them the love of Jesus.
Nagging may take away their appetite for the Word.

Do I pray every day for each family member?
To keep us united I must do everything possible.
God will take care of the impossible.

Do I practice patience, a prime element of love?
I know I'm not perfect. God loves me anyway.
I must not expect perfection in my loved ones.

Am I polite to my family when we are at home?
Good manners involve more than using the right fork.
They recognize the rights, needs, longings of others.

Do I take time to listen?
Listening is paying attention to what is being said.
A deaf ear is the first symptom of a closed mind.

Do I, if possible, avoid hurting feelings?
Genuine love has firmness and discipline,
but it does not put others down.

Do I give constructive criticism in a kind way—
at the right time, not in angry moments?
It must not be given in front of other people.

When there is a dispute, do I speak in love?
When two agree about everything, one is unnecessary.
I can disagree strongly without being disagreeable.

Am I willing to forgive seventy times seven?
Daily irritations and problems offer plenty of occasions.
I must not keep a record of wrongs or dig up the past.

Do I keep in touch with family members not nearby?
Communication is an important ingredient in love.
Often it takes only a small investment of time and effort.

People who feel loved will radiate love.
Love learned at home will touch many other lives.
Love begins at home but does not end there.
Love never ends.

Let God Love You

God's action often depends on our reaction.
He does not depend on us to trigger His behavior.
God always makes the first move.

"Repent, and be baptized. . . .
you will receive the gift of the Holy Spirit."
(Acts 2.38)
"Believe in the Lord Jesus,
and you will be saved." (Acts 16:31)
"Draw near to God
and he will draw near to you." (James 4:8 RSV)
"Humble yourselves before the Lord
and he will exalt you." (James 4:10 RSV)
"Come to me, all who labor and are heavy laden,
and I will give you rest." (Matthew 11:28 RSV)

God has rich benefits to give us.
Anxiously He waits to pour His love into our hearts.
He is able to give us more than we are able to ask.

The Lord could bless us without our cooperation.
Often He does.
Yet for some reason at times He will not act
until we use the strength He gives us.

Our Lord does not force Himself upon us.
He says, *"Behold, I stand at the door and knock;*
if any one hears my voice and opens the door,
I will come in to him and eat with him,
and he with me." (Revelation 3:20 RSV)

When we respond to His love,
we welcome Him and His gifts into our lives.

Take Charge

I cannot choose how others treat me.
I can choose how I will respond.
Others do not make me lose my temper.
I lose it because of what they say or do.
My own weakness makes me lose it.

To blame others for my responses
is to admit I've lost self-control.
I imply that I am a helpless victim
without a free will, acted upon by outside forces.

What others do does affect me.
Sometimes it's possible and wise to avoid those
who annoy, frustrate, discourage, disgust me.
But often I must work with or live near them.

I can pray for these people.
That improves my attitude.
I can pray for myself. That improves my aptitude.
I must ask Jesus to control me,
make me more like Him.
What is impossible for me is "Himpossible."

Jesus loves me and accepts me for what I am.
But He wants me to change, grow, improve.
I must make a real effort to take charge of my life.
His Holy Spirit living in me will enable me.
"For it is God who works in you to will and to act
according to his good purpose." (Philippians 2:13)

Think Good Things

We are what we think.
What we think depends on how we process
all we hear, see, read and experience—
how we respond to all that is said and done to us.

We cannot control the words and deeds of others.
We can modify the influence they have upon us.

Usually we are careful not to contaminate our bodies
by putting into our mouths what is polluted or harmful.
It is even more imperative that we avoid
feeding garbage to our minds.

Many writers of books, magazines, movies, TV programs
feature violence, lust, greed and corruption.
They would have us believe that bad is good
and evil is normal, exciting and rewarding.

It is up to us to refuse to contaminate our minds.
We don't have to read and look at all that is offered.
We must love ourselves enough to protect ourselves.

To counteract bad thoughts that reach through to us,
we ought daily to put in a supply of good thoughts.
We need to read God's Word and meditate upon it.
*"And the peace of God, which transcends all
understanding, will guard your hearts and your minds in
Christ Jesus. . . .
Whatever is true . . . noble . . . right . . . pure . . . lovely
. . . admirable . . . excellent . . . praiseworthy . . . think
about such things."* (Philippians 4:7-8)

Look at the Bright Side

Every life has dark colors and bright ones.
We select which one we will emphasize.
Our choice determines our character
and the influence we have on those around us.
We restrict
    by grumbling about what cannot be done;
we EXPAND
    by setting goals to be reached with God's help.
We discourage
    by complaining about what is lacking;
we ENCOURAGE
    by thanking God for all He has given us.
We sadden
    by remembering what has been lost;
we CONSOLE
    by reminding of what is still left.
We depress
    by concentrating on what is ugly in the world;
we CHEER
    by doing what we can to beautify the world.
We defeat
    by dwelling on our failure;
we CHANGE
    by receiving God's forgiveness
    and using the strength He offers.

*Be imitators of God, therefore,
as dearly loved children and
live a life of love, just as
Christ loved us and gave himself
up for us as a fragrant offering
and sacrifice to God.*

Ephesians 5:1-2

Love Isn't Easy

"A friend in need is a pest!"
This desk plaque must spare its owner some requests.

It may express the way we all feel at times.
Even those of us who take seriously
God's command to love our neighbor
sometimes find it very difficult to do.

Opportunities to serve often come
at what seems the most inopportune time.
Yet the person in need whose path crosses ours
may be God's interruption.

We do not have to do everything people ask of us,
nor give all that is requested.
We need to consider wisely and prayerfully:
what is the truly loving thing to do in this case?

Those we serve may not be grateful.
Instead of the role of hero or heroine
we may find we've been made to play the fool.
Doing it for Jesus' sake helps ease the pain.

One hindrance to serving the Lord
is that we look for special things to do.
While we await some noble task,
we might recall that Jesus "took a towel . . ."

Our Lord gave us an example.
He took the form of a servant.
How did people respond to His love?
Some of them nailed Him to a cross!

That's the risk we take
when we conform to His image.
If we want to be like Jesus,
we'd better look good on wood.

My Duty

Love
is not
God's hope,
His wish or
my option.

Love
is God's
command!

Love
is more
than emotion.
It's an action verb!

Lord,
I need
Your help
to improve my
love ability.

Witness Where You Are

How did you come to consciously know Jesus?
Probably you were introduced to Him
by a relative, friend, pastor or teacher.
God rarely converts without human agents.

People do not save souls; only the Holy Spirit does.
He depends on us to be His witnesses.
We are to testify what Jesus has done
and is doing in our lives.

Jesus says: go to all the world making disciples.
The world starts right where we are.
Each of us has the responsibility to ask:
What on earth am I doing for heaven's sake?

How do you feel when two people come to your door
to share their religious convictions?
If they do not believe Jesus is God,
they represent a false religion.

Do you see them only as an interruption,
wish they would take off and leave you alone?
Or do you see them as poor lost souls
who need to know Jesus, the only way to heaven?

Do you stand there with tied tongue
or bluntly reply, "I'm not interested"?
Or do you see them as a God-given opportunity
to tell the good news of Jesus' love?

We may have difficulty expressing our faith
because we so seldom talk about Jesus.
We fear we might fail to be convincing.
Jesus doesn't ask us to be successful—only faithful.

We should not speak of faith in general terms:
"I believe in God." (So does Satan.)
"I believe in the Bible." (So do some cultists.)
"I belong to a church." (So do a lot of unbelievers.)

We really cannot talk about our faith
unless we talk about Jesus Christ.
It is upon our relation with Him
that our eternity depends! So we exalt Jesus!

With love and assurance say something like this:
"I don't love God as I should.
I don't love myself or others as I ought.
Yet, I know God loves me very much.

"God had His own Son die to pay for my sin.
I trust in Jesus; therefore I know I have eternal life.
If I were to die this very day,
I'm sure I'd be with Jesus forever.

"Such confidence gives me strength for this life.
Jesus is my best Friend; He comforts and protects me.
He guides me in the decisions I make.
His love gives me joy, peace, security!"

We don't have to answer all questions,
or solve all problems that are posed.
We are not to argue—just tell what we know.
That we can do. The Holy Spirit will enable us!

We ought to pray for those with whom we share our faith.
It may take years for God to penetrate their hearts.
Perhaps we'll never know what good our words have done.
Our duty is not to win—but to witness.

What's in a Name?

"God's last name is not Dammit!"
That's bumper sticker wisdom.

We've been given the Ten Commandments.
One is *"You shall not misuse the name of the Lord
your God."* (Exodus 20:7)

God doesn't need a name to identify Himself.
There are no other gods!
We need a name for Him so we can talk about Him.
Moses asked God what He should be called.
God said, *"I AM."* (Exodus 3:14)

Some of God's names show what He is like:

Holy One	God Almighty	Eternal God
Living God	Most High	King of kings

Many names tell about His relation to us:

Creator	Lord	Judge
Redeemer	Good Shepherd	Everlasting Father

God demonstrated His love for us in Jesus,
whose names reveal what He is for us:

Savior	Door	Prince of Peace
Lamb of God	Word	Bread of Life
Immanuel	Way	Resurrection and Life

The intimacy of God's love is shown in names
of God's Holy Spirit:

Counselor	Spirit of Life	Spirit of Grace
Comforter	Spirit of Wisdom	Helper

What's in God's name?

POWER!
Peter said to a lame man, *"In the name of Jesus Christ of Nazareth, walk."* (Acts 3:6b)
The man jumped to his feet and began to walk.

PRAYER POWER!
"You may ask me for anything in my name, and I will do it." (John 14:14)

PRAISE POWER!
"From the rising of the sun to the place where it sets the name of the Lord is to be praised." (Psalm 113:3)

SAVING POWER!
". . . that you may believe that Jesus is the Christ, the Son of God, and that by believing you may have life in his name." (John 20:31)

Our God is great!
He loves us more than we can ever imagine.
His name is holy!
We should speak His name with reverence.
Proclaim it with joy!

God's Name Is Holy

Almighty God,
Creator of heaven and earth!
Your names are wonderful!
They tell me about You
and how much You love me.

Thank You for allowing me to
come into Your throne room.
You are Lord of lords and King of kings!
Yet You want me to call You "Father."
What an honor!
Thank You!

I pray in Jesus' name,
drawing upon His credit.
What a privilege!
Thank You!

Because I was baptized in Your name,
I am Your child.
I bear the name of Christian.
What a responsibility!
Thank You!

Enable me to:
protest when others misuse Your name,
speak Your name with boldness,
bring glory to Your name.

Your name is You!

Strength to Forgive

Lord,
You are an expert forgiver.
I'm a failure.

Someone hurt me so badly I haven't been able to forgive.
You know everything. You know what happened.
He never said, "I'm sorry."
Why should I feel guilty? He's the guilty party!

I've tried to shelve my feelings.
They only gnaw at my conscience.
Help me see anything I might have
said or done to create the problem.

I thought it would be a sign of weakness
to say, "I forgive you."
Now I realize it takes real strength—
more strength than I have.

Help!
I need Your power to do what I must do.

Give me the courage to say, "I forgive you,"
and then to let go of my grievances.
Maybe he won't accept my forgiveness.
That's his problem, not mine.
He's accountable to You—just as I am.
Lord, bless him. Forgive him.

I promise to act as soon as possible.
The longer I wait, the harder it gets.

Please help me to forgive.
I need Your forgiveness!

Love Forgives

If we do not forgive, our faith is fake!
Unforgivingness carries the death penalty!
*"If you do not forgive men their sins,
your Father will not forgive your sins."* (Matthew 6:15)

If we find it impossible to forgive those who hurt us,
it means we don't see ourselves realistically.
We act as though we never sin,
or that our sin is not a serious matter.

Sometimes we confuse forgiving with condoning.
God does not condone; He forgives.
He hates sin but loves the sinner.

To forgive is not to excuse.
God doesn't say, "I know you didn't mean it
or couldn't help it, so you're really not to blame."

God says, "You did wrong!
'The wages of sin is death.' (Romans 6:23)
xBut Jesus died for you. I forgive you, accept you."

The Bible does not say: forgive and forget.
Forgetting may be impossible; at times it's wrong.
We are the total of our experiences.
Our yesterdays have made us what we are today.
To bury our feelings of hurt may only cause
them to go underground to spring up in harmful ways.

We store our memories in the attic of our mind.
How we use them is what counts.

Do we keep score of wrongs done to us,
wallowing in self-pity?
or waiting for a chance to get even?

To tell someone, "I forgive you,"
shares God's love with that person.
It might change his or her life.

It's not always possible to express forgiveness.
The one who hurt us may be dead and gone.
Or we may not know his or her identity or whereabouts.

We can:
    Tell God we forgive that person.
    Confess our failure to forgive. Repent.
    Turn over to Him our feelings of hate and bitterness.
    Accept His forgiving love.
Then we experience cleansing. We are whole.

The greatest benefit comes to the forgiver.
When we forgive, we free ourselves from the
shackles of grudge and resentment.
We unload the misery that weighs on our mind
and is a heavy burden on our soul.

How difficult it is for us to forgive!
How fantastic is the forgiving love of God!

Sick Servant

Lord,
I'm sick and tired of being sick and tired!
Life is so short; it's zapping by
while I mope around and watch.
Please make me well again.

You know I want to serve You.
Of what use is a sick servant?
How can I make the world better
when I can't even do my own chores?

Forgive me for taking good health for granted.
Usually I've made plans far ahead:
next week, next month I'll do this or that.
I must remember to add, "God willing . . ."

Thank You for the doctors, nurses,
modern medicine, equipment and technicians
You've used to heal me and many others.
Keep me thankful as I fill out insurance forms.

Thank You for family and friends.
They have their own pressures to deal with.
Their needs must come before my wants, and yet
I must accept their offers of help with gratitude.

Give me grace to listen to others' troubles
and sense enough not to ramble on about my own.
I'm telling only You about my frustrations.
It's great to know You listen and care!

You comfort me in all my troubles,
so that I can comfort those
in any trouble with the comfort
I myself have received from You. (from 2 Corinthians 1:4)

Take Heart

"Don't you care?"
the disciples cried out to Jesus in panic
as troubles beyond their control overwhelmed them.

God's children are not immune from misfortune.
"In this world you will have trouble.
But take heart!" (John 16.33b)

Why is there evil in the world?
Because Satan is here.
We do not know why a loving God tolerates evil.
We must believe God does not make mistakes.

Our heavenly Father doesn't send tragedies.
He can use them to make us the best He intended us to be.
To eliminate our problems would limit our potential.
If there is no struggle, there is no strength.

When the storms of life close in on us,
we are tempted to cry out, "Why? Why me? Why now?"
Faith moves us to also ask, "What can I learn from this?"
As we plead with God, "Lessen my problem,"
we add, "Teach me a lesson from the problem."

One thing we can learn from trouble is compassion.
Since we understand what suffering is like,
we are in a better position
to share God's love with those who are hurting.

Troubles can be opportunities.
Though they arrive disguised as something bad,
they can help us grow and redirect our lives.

To Each His Own

God doesn't mass produce people.
Each of us is a unique creation.
God deals with us as individuals—not one big group.
Every person has his/her own experience with God.
We must not try to fit others into the mold
of what we are, what we feel or how we worship.

God's ancient people were told to show
reverence for Him in a variety of ways:

"The Lord is in his holy temple;
let all the earth keep silence before him."
(Habakkuk 2:20 RSV)
"Sing to him, sing praises to him,
tell of all his wonderful works!" (Psalm 105:2 RSV)

"Clap your hands, all peoples!
Shout to God with loud songs of joy!" (Psalm 47:1 RSV)

"Praise him with the sounding of the trumpet,
praise him with the harp and lyre,
praise him with tambourine and dancing,
praise him with the strings and flute,
praise him with the clash of cymbals,
praise him with resounding cymbals." (Psalm 150:3-5)

Various gestures were used to indicate respect.
Sometimes people stood before the Lord.
They bowed, knelt or lay prostrate on the ground.
They lifted up their arms. At times they wept.

We must be careful not to judge one another.
Instead we should be patient, understanding and considerate.
We can learn from one another if we don't limit each other.

The important thing is not which instruments we use,
nor the type of songs we sing in praise,
nor whether we fold our hands or hold them high.

The Lord does not prescribe a certain ritual for us.
He is interested in our hearts. He wants faith and love.

"The Lord does not look
at the things man looks at.
Man looks at the outward appearance,
but the Lord looks at the heart." (1 Samuel 16:7b)

Comforting Words

"Fear not, for I have redeemed you;
I have called you by name; you are mine. . . .
I will be with you;
and when you pass through the rivers,
they will not sweep over you. . . .
For I am the Lord, your God,
the Holy One of Israel, your Savior.

Since you are precious and honored in my sight,
and because I love you . . .

Do not be afraid, for I am with you. . . .
Forget the former things;
do not dwell on the past.

. . . You have burdened me with your sins
and wearied me with your offenses.
I, even I, am he who blots out
your transgressions, for my own sake,
and remembers your sins no more."

> God's message to you through
> Isaiah 43: 1, 2, 3, 4, 5, 18, 24, 25

Week-long Service

Lord,
I come into Your presence on Sunday morning.
>You've been with me every day—guiding and guarding.
>You know what I do, think and feel.

I come to Your house partly out of habit and duty.
>Help me regard worship as a privilege and pleasure,
>like the psalmist to rejoice and be glad.

I praise You for Your wonderful deeds.
>I must remember to thank You daily for my blessings.
>My life should be worry-free all week long.

With my offering I praise and thank You.
>All that I own must be used wisely.
>I'm accountable to You for everything I am and have.

Here I allow my mind to dwell on Your great truths.
>Let them permeate my thinking throughout the week.
>You are for me! Who can be against me!

Again I'm reminded of the good news that Jesus loves me.
>When I leave the church, I enter the mission field.
>I must share the good news with others.

The worship service won't end with the benediction.
>That's just the beginning of a week of service.
>What I do for others I am really doing for You.

Moses' face was shining after an encounter with You.
>May my light shine before men,
>that they may see my good deeds
>and praise You, my Father in heaven.

Word Power

Words
enable
us to influence other lives.

Angry,
bitter
words assault the mind and spirit.

Insults,
criticism
shrink the ego and warp the personality.

Praise
motivates
people to rise to full potential.

Needed,
cherished,
encouraging words build up self-esteem.

Soothing,
comforting
words bring a message of God's goodness.

Words
reveal
the measure of love in our own heart.

Believing Is Seeing

Sometimes only what I see, hear and touch seems real.
I can see my body, hear my voice.
I cannot see my spirit.
Yet that is more real.

My flesh, bones and hair are only packaging.
It is my responsibility to take good care of them.
This earthsuit is the only one I'll get.
It must last a lifetime!

My spirit will last for eternity!
How that should be nurtured and cared for daily!

I'm a spiritual being having a human experience.
One day my body will die. Someone will bury it.
But the real me won't be in it.
That will have moved out.
I will have gone to be with my Jesus forever.
One day He will transform my dead body
to be like His glorious body.

Once the Son of God left His Father's heavenly home.
He clothed Himself in human flesh.
His life was perfect—always pleasing to the Father.
Yet men rejected Jesus, tortured and crucified Him.

His death was a horrible miscarriage of justice.
It was also a well-planned sacrifice.
*"For God loved the world so much that he gave
his only Son so that anyone who believes in him
shall not perish but have eternal life."* (John 3:16 TLB)

Because I believe Jesus died for me, He is my Savior.
I see Him as Lord. I follow Him.
I have eternal life. He lives with me now.
I'll live with Him always.

That's real!
That's what life is all about!

I'm Loved to Love

Lord,
You love me!
That's a great, incredible fact!

Jesus,
You proved
Your love with an act of love.

You
became man.
You suffered humiliation, crucifixion.

This
You did
to make me acceptable in Your sight.

You
loved me
before I did. Because You do, I can.

Help
me see myself
as an important instrument of Your love.

Give
me the will
and courage to share Your love with others.

Focus on Jesus

Lord Jesus,
help me focus my eyes upon You!
You are my hope and my salvation!
You are the light at the end of a dark tunnel!

Sorrows and problems surround me.
They make me gloomy and fearful.
When I concentrate on them, shadows darken my way.

Conditions don't make me what I am.
They reveal what I am.
I cannot always change or arrange my circumstances.
I can decide how to react to what happens.
Enable me to be not bitter but better,
not a fault-finder but a faith-lifter.

You did not change or arrange circumstances
to avoid pain and suffering in Your life on earth.
You endured the worst—for my sake.
You were crushed for my iniquities;
the punishment that brought me peace was upon You,
and by Your wounds I am healed.

You are my Savior! How much You love me!
I am convinced that nothing will separate me
from Your love. You have room in Your heart for me.
I come to You with all my frustrations and grief.
You will work for my good in all these things.

Though troubles surround me,
with Your arms around me I'll carry on.

All or Nothing

Lord,
You love me! You're my heavenly Father!
Your Son was sacrificed for me,
so You can forgive and accept me.
How these thoughts warm my heart!

You know I don't want any other gods besides You.
I don't want to make an idol or bow down to one.
I long to keep You number one in my life.
At quiet times like this I concentrate on You.

But I can't do that all the time.
Often I'm so busy with work, family duties,
church activities, volunteering and recreation
I don't take time even to think of You.

I am jolted by this statement in Your Word:
*"The Lord your God is a consuming fire,
a jealous God."* (Deuteronomy 4:24)
You expect full-time commitment—all or nothing!

All that I am and have are gifts from You—
even my chores and responsibilities.
Help me not to be so concerned about Your gifts
that I fail to keep You on the throne in my life.

*"My command
is this:
Love
each other
as I have
loved you."*
John 15:12

Busy! Busy!

Lord,
I'm so busy!
I don't have much time
to spend with You today.
Forgive me. I'm sure You understand.

Life ought not
be a search for happiness.
Yet we must be clothed, fed.
We need to earn money to do that.

Seek first
His kingdom and righteousness.
Lord, You are my king, and yet
I must concern myself with earthly things.

I cannot
be so heavenly minded
that I'm no earthly good.
I need to take care of myself and others.

Help me remember
all things are gifts from You.
You give me strength to serve
the loved ones You've placed in my care.

Keep me mindful
that my blessings from You
must not distract me from
concentrating on You and Your great love.

May I see
I can be serving You when I
perform my duties faithfully
whether at church, home or place of work.

As I strive
to do what is urgent today,
help me not neglect the important.
Keep me aware of Your constant companionship.

*"The only thing
that counts
is faith
expressing itself
through love."*
Galatians 5:6b

You Belong to Jesus

Do you believe in Jesus?
Do you believe He died for you? for you personally?
If you trust in Jesus as your Savior,
you are a Christian, a little Christ.
He has put His stamp of ownership upon you.
You belong to Jesus!

Jesus unites us with Himself.
We are *in Christ,* in union with Him, tied to Him.
"If anyone is in Christ, *he is a new creation;
the old has gone, the new has come!"* (2 Corinthians 5:17)
Personal contact with Jesus alters everything!
We become new people!

Jesus brings unity between God and us.
The Lord is holy. He demands perfection of us.
Christ died for our imperfections!
"In him *we have redemption through his blood,
the forgiveness of sins, in accordance with the
riches of God's grace that he lavished on us . . ."*
(Ephesians 1:7-8a)

Our relation to Jesus
makes us acceptable to the Almighty!
"In him *and through faith* in him *we may
approach God with freedom and confidence."*
(Ephesians 3:12)
Jesus makes it possible for us to call His Father
our Father.

We have a connection with the Source.
Jesus is the Vine; we are the branches.
He supplies the nourishment we require.
If we remain in Him, all He offers is ours.
We need only surrender ourselves:
"Take me, Lord. I'm Yours!"

Jesus Is Yours

There is an appalling difference between God's expectations
and the way you live your life.
By yourself it is impossible for you to please God.

Fortunately, you don't have to earn forgiveness.
It's there if you'll receive it.
It is a free gift from God Himself.
He is the Giver. He is the Gift.

Quietly, simply, without any fuss,
Jesus came down to where you are
so that You may live where He is!

Holy Communion reminds you that Jesus loves you
personally.
"This is my body given for you. . . .
This cup is the new covenant in my blood,
which is poured out for you." (Luke 22:19-20)

As you swallow those elements, they become part of you.
Jesus becomes part of you also in a spiritual sense.

"He is able to save completely
those who come to God through him,
because he always lives to intercede for them."
(Hebrews 7:25)
Jesus isn't finished with you yet.
He still pleads for you.

Jesus says, "Follow me."
Follow Him. Imitate Him.
Let Him speak and act through you.
Have His attitude toward other people.

You and Jesus belong to each other.
You are His. He is yours!

"The Lord himself
goes before you
and will be with you;
he will never leave you
nor forsake you.
Do not be afraid;
do not be discouraged.

". . . Let the beloved of the Lord
rest secure in him,
for he shields him all day long,
and the one the Lord loves
rests between his shoulders."

(Deuteronomy 31:8; 33:12)

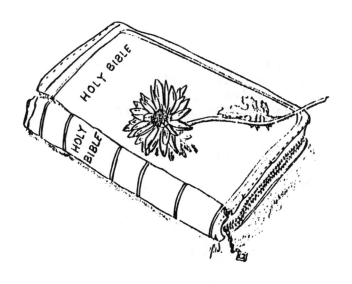

The Good Shepherd

Lord,
I do believe you are my Shepherd.
You tell me to follow.
I'm trying to do that.
But at times it's very hard.

At first I was so confident.
I expected to lie down in green pastures,
live a life of ease beside quiet waters,
with an overflowing cup of blessings.

The road on which You're leading me
is so full of rocks it's hard for me to walk.
I've stumbled and bruised myself.
The brambles make progress difficult.

You get so far ahead of me
because You keep on going forward.
I dillydally along the way
looking for easier paths to take.

Why is it I shy away from dark places?
Feel threatened by deep valleys?
It's because I'm not close enough to You, Lord.
I've focused on myself rather than on You.

You are the good Shepherd.
You laid down Your life for me.
Surely You are leading me in the right way,
guarding me from the evil one.

I don't understand the way I'm being led.
But I know You. I know You love me.
You're taking me to Your eternal home.
Help me follow in Your footsteps.

Comfort for God's People

"See, the Sovereign Lord comes with power,
and his arm rules for him.

"He tends his flock like a shepherd;
He gathers the lambs in his arms
and carries them close to his heart;
he gently leads those that have young.

"The Lord is the everlasting God,
the Creator of the ends of the earth.
He will not grow tired or weary,
and his understanding no one can fathom.
He gives strength to the weary
and increases the power of the weak.

"Those who hope in the Lord
will renew their strength.
They will soar on wings like eagles;
they will run and not grow weary;
they will walk and not be faint."

(Isaiah 40:10, 11, 28, 29, 31)

The Church Is You

People looking around for a new church home
most often choose one that is friendly.
Who is responsible for friendliness?
The pastor? The ushers? The greeters? Yes!
It is also your responsibility. You are the church!

Do you have the joy of Jesus in your heart?
If so, let your face know it—and show it!
Smile at people and be friendly.

Though you may be shy, introduce yourself
to someone you haven't met before.
Perhaps that person also is shy—and lonely.

Do not allow yourself to be so intent on
talking with friends that you ignore visitors.
You can call your friends later.

Be a friend by setting a good example.
Do not read the bulletin or announcement sheet
when others are singing, praying, listening.
This distracts those around you.
How it must offend the Lord!

Worship Him wholeheartedly,
but don't act as if people near you are invisible.
Public worship is personal but not private.

If you notice that someone is missing,
be a self-appointed committee of one
to make a phone call and say, "I missed you."

If you learn that a member is ill or in special need,
let him or her know you'll pray about it.
Also offer a listening ear and a helping hand.

When people return after a long absence,
instead of embarrassing them,
tell them you're glad to see them.

God's children come in all ages, colors,
shapes and sizes with varying degrees of
intelligence, ability, education, wealth, charm.
God loves variety!
Never act as if some don't count.

You are the church.
If you fail to show love,
the church fails to show love.
When the church fails to love,
some people may be turned away
and never know God's great Gift of love.

The Church Loves

"I did not feel anyone cared
if I was there or not."
That's what most people said
when asked why they stopped going to church.

Our main reason for church-going
is to worship the Lord—
to express our love for Him
with thanksgiving and praise.

If we say we love God
but don't love the people around us,
we cannot really love God.
That's serious business!

The congregation is one branch of God's family.
We are children of the heavenly Father—
a support system for one another.
Our worship service is a family reunion.

We come as we are—with failures and victories,
a sense of frustration and joy of fulfillment.
All of us require forgiveness.
Everybody needs encouragement.

We weep with those who weep,
rejoice with those who rejoice.
We pray for one another and for others.
Burdens are shouldered; blessings shared.

Each of us needs to be refreshed by God's love
and to experience His love through others.
Love is God's formula for solving our problems.
Each of us can help make the love of God more real.

Take Care of Yourself

Love is not a theory. It is down-to-earth stuff!

The most startling truth God has revealed
about Himself is that He loves me!
Jesus came down to earth to demonstrate it.

"If you love me," says Jesus, *"you will obey
what I command."* (John 14:15)
One of God's commands is: You shall not murder.
As a child I learned this means
I should not hurt or harm my neighbor's body,
but help and befriend him in every bodily need.

What about me? I'm primarily responsible for myself.
When I injure my body with willful or careless neglect,
that's a sin! I am to love my neighbor and myself.
I don't love myself by hurting my health.

Dear Lord, thank You for loving me.
Help me love myself.
Forgive me for often disobeying You by not
practicing good health habits.
With Your help I will:
• get the proper amount of rest and exercise.
• eat things that are good for me and avoid what's bad.
• regard my doctor as Your instrument if he tells me to
  reduce my weight, cholesterol, blood pressure.
• not pollute my body with harmful substances.
• drive carefully on the highway to prevent accidents.
• always buckle my seatbelt.
• avoid harming myself to look good to others.

I know that my body is the temple of Your Holy Spirit,
who is in me, whom I have received from You!
I am not my own; I was bought with a price.
Therefore I will honor You with my body.

Exercise Faith

What a never-to-be-forgotten experience!
Peter was walking on water!
Then he saw the wind whipping up huge waves around him.
He became frightened and began to sink.
Fear made Peter doubt Jesus' love and power.

Did Jesus commend him and say, "Good try!"? No!
"You of little faith . . . why did you doubt?"
(Matthew 14:31)
Jesus didn't want to destroy Peter's self-confidence.
He wanted Peter to develop more God-confidence.

Faith saves. Faith rests on Jesus' love and power.
We rely on Him, not on our goodness.
We trust in Jesus and Jesus alone for salvation.
Because He laid down His life for us, we have eternal life.

Faith is a gift to be exercised.
It enables us to cope with the fears of this world.

We fear the future, the unknown, inadequacy, failure.
Each one fears different dangers, situations.
Fear is normal. Only a fool is afraid of nothing.
God never says we'll have nothing to be afraid of.
He does say, "Fear not. I am with you."

Faith in our ever-present Lord unleashes His power.
Faith empowers us to reach beyond our grasp.
When we extend ourselves to the utmost,
we often discover more energy, skill and endurance
than we ever imagined was in us.

To take a leap of faith is an exhilarating experience.
We give it all we've got and trust Jesus for all He is.

Who? Me?

I know more about what goes on in the White House
than in the white house down my street.
I don't even know the name of that family.

World news bombards me with so many problems—
the hapless, the homeless, the hungry, the hurting.
I pity those people. But it's more than I can deal with.

Forgive me, Lord, for wringing my hands and fretting,
"Why isn't this world a better place?
Why doesn't somebody do something about it?"

Help me remember You expect me to be doing that.
Give me the courage to ask sincerely,
"How can I help make the world a little better place?"

I cannot do everything; I can do certain things.
I cannot be everywhere; I can start where I am.
I cannot help everyone; I can help someone.

You have blessed me, Lord. You've been so good to me.
I bask in the wonderfulness of Your love.
I want to radiate it, reflect it, share it with others.

You want me to go looking for trouble, get involved.
Open my eyes, ears, heart and wallet.
Something good can happen through me today!

Together with God

Lord,
sometimes You tell me to do things
contrary to my common sense.

Help me remember
You not only expect me to do Your will,
but You are in me to do it.

Without me
You will not.

Without You
I cannot.

Now Choose Life

"Lord, help me do with a smile
the things I have to do anyhow."
This prayer posted on her laundry room wall reminds the
young mother the choice is hers, the power is God's.

We do not choose to be born. When. Where.
We do not choose parents or our upbringing.
We do not choose all our circumstances or conditions.
We did not choose God either. He chose us to be His own.

But within all this choicelessness
we do choose how we shall live.
Our attitude toward our challenges and chores
determines what we do about them.

We decide how we will respond to what happens to us:
to be fearful or faithful,
to feel discouraged or determined,
to grumble or to glow.

We decide what is most important to us.
We may magnify trifles and trifle with magnitudes.
Or we can glorify God for His wonderful love and power
and allow Him to use us in His plan to love the world.

God is the source of all the energy in the atom.
He is willing to fill us!
Jesus says, *"I have come that they may have life,
and have it to the full."* (John 10:10)

Therapy of Thanksgiving

When asked, "How are you?"
Betty bubbled, "Marvelous!
The Lord has been so good to me!"
Had she just returned from a cruise?
No. From a hospital. Mastectomy!
An operation dreaded by many women.

She went on with enthusiasm:
"There is so much to be thankful for!
I feel better than I had expected.
Family and friends have been fantastic!
Doctors, nurses, hospital workers were wonderful!

"So many people were praying for me.
Jesus was with me holding me close.
Knowing God was in control put my mind at ease.
Over and over I repeated Bible verses I had memorized:
     'You are precious in my eyes,
     and honored, and I love you.' (Isaiah 43:4 RSV)
     'Fear not, for I am with you.' (Isaiah 41:10 RSV)
     'The Lord is my shepherd.' (Psalm 23.1)
This experience has taught me to be more empathetic
with people who have problems.
I'll do whatever I can to be useful to them."

How could this woman come up so positive
after such a traumatic experience?
She has learned to *"Give thanks in all circumstances."*
(1 Thessalonians 5:18)
That's good therapy!
Concentrating on what is good hastens the healing process.
It also makes a person easier to love.

Faith in God's goodness helps us read love
in even the greatest of evils,
to put the best construction on all God's dealings.
When trouble comes—as it does to every life—
faith enables us to ask, "What love can I see in
this?"

"The life
I live
in the body,
I live
by faith
in the Son of God,
who loved me
and gave himself
for me."
      (Galatians 2:20b)

Handle with Care

"Kiss me again."
No passion here—
just a tender touch of lips on brow.

I laughed and tucked him in
and said, "Good night. I love you."

Did he sense what I didn't know—
that this would be our last farewell?
Soon God would call him home.

Senility had robbed him of
memories, strength, independence, dignity.
It had not diminished his need to be loved.

Thank God for hours we spent together.
They spared regrets that some have known.

After his wife of forty years
had been suddenly snatched away,
Thomas Carlyle wrote in his diary,
"Oh, that I had you yet for five minutes
by my side, that I might tell you all."

How tenderly we should treat our loved ones!
The days of love are short!

God Is Here

The young family traveled for hours to reach the remote park.
Before their picnic lunch the father led them in prayer.
The five-year-old thought for a while and solemnly asked,
"Do you think God knows where we are?"

Have you ever pondered the question,
"Is God really here with me now?"

Sometimes we confine God to certain places—
perhaps the church where we worship Him.
We may limit Him to certain occasions—
mealtimes, bedtimes, troubled times.

Over and over God promises
to be present with His people.
His presence is more than His existence.
Naturally, God is everywhere—for He is God.
His presence with those who love Him
is a special blessing.

He can withdraw His presence.
To the disobedient and unfaithful He said,
*"Because you have turned away from the Lord,
he will not be with you . . ."* (Numbers 14:43)
They had to repent and return.
Then God restored the relationship.

If God seems far away, who do you think moved?
Tell the Lord if His presence doesn't seem real.
Admit you have been doing something wrong—
or failing to do what was right.
Ask God to forgive you. Believe that He has.

God is here—whether you feel His presence or not.
God loves you. He wants to be welcome in your life.
"Come near to God and he will come near to you."
(James 4:8)
Talk with Him informally in scattered moments.
Prayer opens your life to His blessings and influence.
God's presence will give you comfort and courage.

Worship the Lord

The Lord is great and greatly to be praised!
He is far, far beyond our understanding.
The Bible gives us only a limited view of what He is like.

The Supreme Being is all-powerful.
Everything that exists was created by Him—
from microscopic creatures to the far-flung galaxies.
He controls it, all-knowing and present everywhere.

The Lord created us in His own image,
yet we have the capacity to deny Him, defy Him.
Our holy Lord, the Judge of the world,
loves us despite our disobedience.
In Jesus He offers forgiveness and eternal life.

How should we respond? God told His people of old,
"Observe the Sabbath day by keeping it holy."
(Deuteronomy 5:12)

Our wise and loving Father wants us
to take time each week from our workaday schedule
to honor Him—for His glory and our good!

As God's people we gather to worship Him.
"Glorify the Lord with me;
let us exalt his name together." (Psalm 34:3)
We remind ourselves and others of God's greatness.
We thank and praise Him for His loving kindness.
Together we learn His ways so we may walk in His paths.
We pray, sing and fellowship,
serving as a support group for one another.
The worship service is a shared experience.
Yet worship comes from individual hearts.

True worship is more than just attending church.
It is coming before God to show our devotion to Him.
In the splendor of His holiness our sin is more evident.
With humble hearts we ask the Lord to forgive and renew us.

We do not focus merely on ourselves
as poor miserable sinners.
We focus on the Lord our Maker, our forgiving Father.
It is He who saved us and enables us to live as His own.

Our worship service is more than a ceremony.
It should be a celebration!
Our Lord loves us!
We worship Him!

"Above all,
love
each other
deeply,
because
love
covers over
a multitude
of sins."
(1 Peter 4:8)

Live for God

Lord,
make me pure
so others may see
what a wonderful person You've made of me.

Put
me in Your
showroom of saints
to enjoy a life without any complaints.

God's answer:

But
I called you
so others may know
My love shining through you wherever you go.

Life
won't be easy,
but surely will be
a great satisfaction in living for Me.

Facing the Bench

One day I will stand before the Judge!

I don't have to earn His pardon.
I know that I am saved
through the grace of the Lord Jesus.

What amazing love my God has shown me!
He chose me to be His own—
to live in His kingdom forever and ever.

When I meet Jesus face to face, how shall I account
for the way I have responded to His love?

I cannot blame others for what I've done.
I cannot excuse myself because I did only
what everybody else was doing.
I cannot blame God for giving me difficult tasks
or an unpleasant environment in which to do them.

Nor do I want to say, "Lord, You told me to love You
with all my heart and my neighbor as myself.
But since salvation is free, I've squeaked by,
loving You and my neighbor as little as possible."

O Jesus, Your grace is not cheap!
You died for me. Help me live for You!
Enable me to love You more each day and
to transmit Your love to those around me.
Grant that one day I may hear You say,
"Well done, good and faithful servant! . . .
Come and share your master's happiness!" (Matthew 25:23)

"Love is patient,
love is kind.
It does not envy,
it does not boast,
it is not proud.
It is not rude,
it is not self-seeking,
it is not easily angered,
it keeps no record of wrongs.
Love does not delight in evil
but rejoices with the truth.
It always protects, always trusts,
always hopes, always perseveres.
Love never fails."
(1 Corinthians 13:4-8)

Love Is Greatest

Lord Jesus,
I love You.

I want to be like You.
Please fill me with Your love.

Make me patient and kind.
Keep me from being envious or boastful.
Help me never be arrogant or rude.

I will try not to demand my own way.
I will not be easily angered.
I won't keep a record of wrongs done to me.
I won't be happy with evil that happens
but will delight in the truth.

I'm sure You are listening to my prayer.
Thank you for answering.
With Your help I will be stronger, more loving.
I expect miracles!

Give with Love

Our giving "gives us away."
Not what we give, but why we give matters.

Sometimes we donate time, effort, money, materials
because someone else has twisted our arm.
Our heart is not in it. We just want to keep face.
It may do some good—but not for us.

Some people expect their generosity will bribe God.
We don't buy God's mercy with good deeds.
Only the precious blood of Jesus
can make us right with our heavenly Father.

We have been blessed to be a blessing.
We share what we have with God's other children,
because our Father tells us to love them.
What we do for others, we do for Jesus.

Our giving is to be a thankoffering—
a recognition of the love God lavishes upon us.
With David we exclaim, *"Who am I, and who are my people,
that we should be able to give as generously as this?
Everything comes from you, and we have given you only
what comes from your hand."* (1 Chronicles 29:14)

In the Old Testament God told His people
to give the tithe, ten percent of their income.
Tithing is not a New Testament command,
yet God's ancient promise is still valid.
*"Bring the whole tithe . . . and see if I will not throw open
the floodgates of heaven and pour out so much blessing
that you will not have room enough for it."*
(Malachi 3:10)

Those of us who accept God's challenge know
our giving is a token of our trust in the Lord.
Our confidence is in God Himself, not in His blessings.
We cannot outgive God.

Love Gives

In Jesus we see what our heavenly Father is like.
In Jesus we see also what we should be like.

God so loved the world that He gave.
Jesus so loved us that He gave.

We don't love people unless we give.
We demonstrate love by doing something to show it.

At times we say, "It's the thought that counts."
Not always! Often only what we do is real!

To show love takes effort and time.
A note or phone call can brighten someone's day.

An offer of help lightens a heavy load.
A word of encouragement can bring new hope.

A patient, listening ear can tell another:
I have time for you; you're important.

We may do good deeds seething with resentment,
"Who do you think I am? Your slave?"

This may fulfill our obligation of duty,
but not our obligation to love.

By doing loving acts we may eventually
develop loving attitudes.

We do not stack up good deeds to bargain with God.
Our love is a response. He first loved us.

Hearts warmed by God's amazing love
cannot be indifferent to the needs of others.

Love is the unmistakable badge of a Christian.

Shine!

I am
not an insignificant speck of dust
on an unimportant planet in the vastness of space.

I am
a child of my heavenly Father,
made in His image, put here to be a light in the world.

Often
my actions mar the image.
This does not cancel the fact that He is my Father.

When
Moses had been with God,
people around him noticed his face was radiant.

Lord,
give me the power to glow.
Use me to be a bright moment in somebody's day.

Help
me let my light so shine
that people see my good deeds and praise You.

God Always Answers Prayer

Sometimes God says "Yes"
in ways so spectacular
we call them miracles,
or by such ordinary means
we must be alert to notice.

Often God says "Wait."
He knows some things we don't know.
We see only the here and now.
Circumstances may not be right
or we may need to be changed.

At times the Lord says "No,"
not because He doesn't hear,
but because He has a better idea.
If God were always to answer "Yes"
we might be afraid to pray.

The Lord Listens

We communicate with the Lord all the time.
Without conscious thought our actions tell Him:
"I want to please You," or "I can handle this myself."

Our all-wise Creator made us in His image—
capable of talking to Him! or ignoring Him!
He wants us to pray—for our own good.

The King of kings offers to be part of our lives.
He is here—whether we feel His presence or not.
But He doesn't force Himself or His blessings on us.

Jesus says, *"Here I am! I stand at the door and knock.*
If anyone hears my voice and opens the door,
I will come in and eat with him, and he with me."
(Revelation 3:20)

Prayer opens the door of our hearts to the Lord.
It is our response to His love.
He waits to be wanted!

What to Pray

Adoration
> This sets the stage for prayer.
> As we praise God for His greatness and goodness,
> we remind ourselves that the Ruler of creation
> is our loving heavenly Father.
> He is with us, willing to listen and answer.

Confession
> God sees our hearts. He knows we've failed
> to love Him, ourselves and others.
> We need to confess specific sins,
> not just vaguely "all our sins and iniquities."
> If we repent, God is faithful and forgives.
> He is merciful, not because we are deserving,
> but because He is love. That love was costly!
> Jesus died a horrible death to pay for our sins.

Thanksgiving
> We express gratitude for the Lord's amazing grace—
> for our spiritual and temporal gifts.
> Counting our blessings trains us to praise
> and thank God before we ask Him for more and more.

Supplication
> Honestly and simply we can tell all our
> needs, wants, problems, dreams and hopes.
> Nothing is too big or too small for God's attention.
> He will do what we have asked Him to do—
> according to His wise and loving will.
> He is our beautiful Savior who wants us
> to stay in personal touch with Him.

Pray Continually

Most
of the time
I ignore my
vacuum cleaner.

I'm
glad it is
available
whenever I need it.

Lord,
forgive me
for often
treating You this way.

Be Yourself

You are a unique, unrepeatable miracle!

Only two people in all the history of the world
could have been your parents.
The two cells that made you determined
your structure, size, color and other attributes.

There is nobody else exactly like you.
You can be positively identified from a drop of blood,
a strand of hair, a bit of skin or any other tissue.

Your environment and your experiences
have modified, shaped and influenced you.

God knows what is in you, what you are—
all your memories, feelings, thoughts,
likes, dislikes, strengths and weaknesses.

He judges you not by what He has given you,
but by your faithfulness in developing and using it.

He put you where you are at this point in time,
at this stage of your life, for some good reason.

There is a unique role for you to play.
People around you need the love only you can give.

Do the best you can with what you've got
under the circumstances!

*"When
I said,
'My foot
is slipping,'
your love,
O Lord,
supported me."*
(Psalm 94:18)

Strength in Weakness

Faith is not insurance against disaster.
Even those who obey the Lord faithfully
are sometimes beset with severe difficulties.

The apostle Paul had more troubles than most people
because he was the Lord's obedient servant.
Late one night in a dark prison cell *"The Lord
stood near Paul and said, 'Take courage! . . ."* (Acts 23:11)

The Lord did not say, "Cheer up, Paul, nothing
bad will happen to you. Everything will be all right."

Later Paul could write, *"I delight in weaknesses,
in insults, in hardships, in persecutions, in difficulties.
For when I am weak, then I am strong."*
(2 Corinthians 12:10)

Usually we ask God to steer us away from hardships.
We want Him to remove all trials from our lives.
We'd like to have only smooth sailing.
It doesn't work that way.
God's power is made perfect in our weakness.

Some problems come our way because we do God's will.
Most are just our share of life's normal ordeals.
We live with the ever-present possibility of catastrophe.

But we can go on with courage.
Our almighty, loving Father is with us.
He is in us. He is for us.

We will not be crushed.
We will be conquerors through Christ.

The Lord Enables

When the Israelites were thirsty in the desert,
they grumbled to Moses, "Give us water to drink."
God told Moses to bring water out of a rock.
The command seemed ridiculous.
Did God expect Moses to do a miracle?

A crowd of five thousand people had gathered.
Jesus told His disciples, "Give them something to eat."
"We have only five loaves and two fish," they replied.
The instruction seemed absurd.
Did Jesus expect them to perform a miracle?

The angel appeared to Mary the virgin saying,
"You will give birth to a son.
He will be called the Son of the Most High."
"How will this be?" asked Mary.
Did the Lord expect her to perform a miracle?

Moses had only to obey God's command.
The disciples turned over their limited resources.
Mary offered herself—her body, her life—
to bring into the world God's Gift of love.
God would do the miracles!

Our Lord tells us, "Go, make disciples of all nations."
That's a big job—sharing God's love with the world!
Our resources are so limited! Our faith so weak!
How can this be?
Does God expect us to perform a miracle?

We slander God when we say, "You demand too much of me.
You expect more than You give me power to do."
We need only to believe and obey,
turn over to Him what we are and have.
God does the miracles!

Not Guilty!

"Be holy because I, the Lord your God, am holy."
(Leviticus 19:2)
Lord, You are holy.
That's Your very nature.

I can't be holy.
It's not my nature!

"I have the desire to do what is good,
but I cannot carry it out.
For what I do is not the good I want to do;
no, the evil I do not want to do—
this I keep on doing." (Romans 7:18-19)

My sins are deeply personal.
Thank You, Father, for becoming personally
involved in my problem.
You sacrificed Your Son for me.
He bore the eternal consequence of my sin.
You've dropped the charges against me.
The case is closed! I praise and thank You!

Yet I must live with the earthly consequence of my sin.
Some wrongs cannot be undone.
Lost opportunities are gone forever.
I cannot live my life over.
Help me surrender what is left for You to use.
Give me courage to become more like You.

You are a God of forgiveness,
the Inventor of the second chance.
I praise and thank You, Lord!

Joy Is Knowing God's Love

Lord,
You understand my problems
and all that troubles my mind.

I'm sure of Your love.
You've taken care of me
even though the going has been rough.

Please control my tomorrows
as You managed my yesterdays.
Help me to let go and let You.

Joy in life does not depend
on health, family, friends, security.
These have been my bonus from You.

Everything I see and feel
will someday be taken from me.
My oneness with You will go on forever.

*"The
Lord's
unfailing love
and mercy
still continue,*

*Fresh
as the
morning,
as sure
as the
sunrise."*
(Lamentations 3:22-23 TEV)

Hope in the Lord

"All we can do is hope and pray."
That's plenty!
Hope and prayer link us with the loving, living Lord!

Jesus' resurrection assures believers of a certain hope.
We will live with Him forever in His glorious home.
But ours is not just a pie-in-the-sky-by-and-by hope.
It is a down-to-earth tonic affecting not only our spirit
but our mind and body as well. They're interconnected!

"Be strong and take heart,
all you who hope in the Lord." (Psalm 31:24)
David wrote this when his situation seemed hopeless.

Hope is not wishful thinking.
Wishing means just sitting on our hands waiting.
Hope means to see the possible outcome and work for it.
It is a confident expectation that our desire
will be fulfilled, something we long for realized.

Without hope we feel discouraged and despondent.
At times refusal to hope is a decision to die.
If we maintain hope, we have a better chance for survival.
It reminds us that with God all things are possible.

Hope is confidence in God's love, wisdom and power.
When it becomes obvious that our will is not His will,
we yield to His higher wisdom though we cannot
understand.

"May your unfailing love rest upon us, O Lord,
even as we put our hope in you." (Psalm 33:22)

Getting It Together

Dear Lord,
Sometimes I feel like a piece of yarn.
Pulled in so many different directions,
I think I'm coming unwound.

I'm called to give
a little time here,
a piece of life there,
a portion of strength elsewhere.

Help me make right choices,
to use my time and energy wisely.
Enable me to know what You want me to do
and to say "no" to that which sidetracks me.

I know I should spend and be spent.
But I must have time alone with You—
to replenish my store of faith and love
lest I be too poor to give.

Do Not Lose Heart

Nothing stays the same.
Change is the law of life.

We celebrate the changes in bodies of young children.
Changes are welcome milestones in their development.
As we age, we no longer celebrate the changes.
They are unwelcome signs of our deterioration.

When hints of gray slip into our hair,
lines gather around the eyes, and
one part after another ceases to function properly,
we struggle to resist or compensate for the changes.
Most of us don't really want to be young again.
We just want to keep from getting old.

Changes in our bodies are reminders of our mortality.
Life is terminal from the moment we're born.
Nobody gets out of here alive!

Our attitude must not be gloom and doom.
The present body need not be a drag on the spirit.
*"We do not lose heart. Though outwardly we are
wasting away, yet inwardly we are being renewed
day by day."* (2 Corinthians 4:16)

Each of us can be certain.
    God loves me just as I am.
    He has some purpose for my life—
    no matter what age I am or stage I'm in.

    I know my Redeemer lives!
    Because He lives, I, too, will live—
    either here on earth—or in His radiant presence!

    Death is not the last page of the book.
    The story of life has a happier ending.
    I shall see God!

*"We love him,
because he first loved us."*
(1 John 4.19 KJV)

Parents Share God's Love

It is our privilege
to bring children into the world.

It is our responsibility
to feed, clothe, care for them.

It is our duty
to train, discipline, educate them.

It is our joy
to share God's love and nurture their faith.

We must guide them,
then let them set their own goals.

We need to encourage,
then let them dream their own dreams.

It is up to us
to help them grow, then let them go.

*"Teach a child how he should live,
and he will remember it all his life."*
(Proverbs 22:6 TEV)

Speak in Love

Sometimes the most loving thing to say
is absolutely nothing.

Just before leaving, someone says in panic,
"I can't find my keys!"
That's the poorest time for words of wisdom,
"Why don't you put them in the proper place?"

When a little child falls and skins a knee, to say,
"I told you not to run around," adds insult to injury.

Our words of wisdom may be very sound,
but they are not very loving.
They hurt rather than help
because they come at the wrong time.

People in crises need a helping hand,
not a piece of our mind.

Lord, with my vast store of good advice,
it often seems a pity not to share it.
Let me speak the truth only when
it's the loving thing to do.
You give me encouragement and help
even when I've made stupid mistakes.
Help me treat others as You treat me.

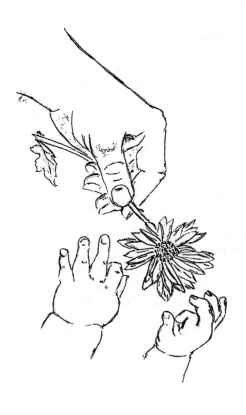

110

Encourage One Another

"Grandma, you make the best turkey soup in the world."
That remark made the effort of soup-making worthwhile!

To know one is appreciated warms the heart.
It lifts a tired spirit, brings out the best in us.

We were created with a longing for acceptance.
"Encourage one another and build each other up."
(1 Thessalonians 5:11)

Self-confidence is built up by compliments.
We help others become what they are capable of being.

Compliments are not flattery or buttering others up.
They are words spoken in sincerity and with love.

Praise lets another know: you are important. You count.
What you are and what you do make a difference.

Lord, enable me to see good in other people
and give me the grace to tell them so.

Focus on God's Goodness

"I don't pray about my problems before going to bed.
Those I discuss with the Lord in the morning.
At night I go over my reasons for giving thanks."

The woman who said this has learned it robs her
of sleep to rehearse details of her troubles.
She falls asleep counting blessings instead of sheep.

We reinforce our faith when we focus on God's goodness.
*"Thou dost keep him in perfect peace, whose mind is
stayed on thee, because he trusts in thee."*
(Isaiah 26:3 RSV)

We can pour out before the Lord all that distresses us
whatever hour of day or night suits our needs.
God is always near, willing to listen, able to help.

Jesus promises, *"Come to me, all you who are weary and
burdened, and I will give you rest."* (Matthew 11:28)
Our loving Lord is greater than any problem we have!

"And we know
that in all things
God works for the good
of those who love him,
who have been called
according to his purpose.

What, then, shall we say
in response to this?
If God is for us,
who can be against us?"
(Romans 8:28, 31)

Newly Elected!

O Lord,
I've been elected to an office!
What have I gotten myself into?
I don't know if I can handle this!
I'd rather be just one of the members.

After the nominating committee approached me,
I talked it over with You.
It seemed You were telling me, "Go ahead, say 'Yes'!"
That was easy. Now I have second thoughts.

I don't know what I'm going to do!
But I'm sure You know what You're going to do.
You won't ever leave me in the lurch.
You'll always be near to give me courage.

My weaknesses make me feel inadequate.
Help me remember: "When I am weak, then I am strong."
My wit's end is the beginning of Your wisdom.
I do not serve alone. You are my Partner.

My job will take prayer, preparation, perspiration.
You won't do the work for me.
Just hand me the tools.
With You by my side I'll do the best I can.

Take Time Out

God lets us ignore Him if that's what we want.

Most of the time we don't consciously disobey God.
We simply don't pay attention to Him.

What hinders us from thinking about Him
is our devotion to people and things.

Common sense shouts loud and clear:
What will we eat? What will we wear?
Bills must be paid, the shopping done.

Our heavenly Father knows we must attend to these.
He will enable us to fulfill our responsibilities.
But more important is our relationship with Him.
He loves us. He wants to communicate with us.

We can talk with God while we are on the run.
But if we talk only when we are running,
we may not hear what He's trying to tell us.

Even the psalmist disciplined himself.
"Praise the Lord, O my soul."
We need to take ourselves by the scruff of the neck,
"Come on, soul. Remember who's in control!"

Taking time to spend alone with God in the morning
and in moments throughout the day brings us peace.
To remind ourselves of God's goodness and promises
prepares us for whatever the day may bring.

It is far better to prepare and prevent
than to repair and repent.

Rejoice in the Lord Always

"If I enjoy it, it's illegal, immoral or fattening."
Such logic implies God doesn't want us to enjoy ourselves.

God *"provides us with everything for our enjoyment,"*
(1 Timothy 6:17b)
but in His wisdom and love He gives us limitations.

The Lord doesn't want to take the joy out of life.
He designed us for joy. Joy is our birthright.

Our problem is that often we emphasize His gifts
and neglect to concentrate on the gift of Himself.

Our greatest joy doesn't come from earthly blessings.
Joy is not dependent on life's circumstances.

Joy is a deep inner feeling of well-being
that comes from knowing we are dearly loved by God.

Joy is knowing Jesus as Savior and Friend,
experiencing the comfort and confidence of His
presence.

When the Holy Spirit comes to live within us,
joy is one of the fruits He produces in our lives.

Joy is not just for good and happy times.
It lasts though nothing goes right and all seems lost.

*"Though the fig tree does not bud
and there are no grapes on the vines,
though the olive crop fails
and the fields produce no food,
though there are no sheep in the pen
and no cattle in the stalls,
yet I will rejoice in the Lord,
I will be joyful in God my Savior."*
(Habakkuk 3:17-18)

Power of One

What can I do about it?
I'm only one among so many!

Once in a while one vote decides
who wins and who loses an election.

One atheist can so twist democratic justice
that a nation's schools are closed to prayer.

One alcoholic brings trouble to a family for generations
and tragedy to those met by accident on the highway.

One spark plug whips up enthusiasm in volunteers
to clean up their city and make it beautiful.

One wise, praying parent through well-trained children
blesses many, many other people for years to come.

One person can tell another about Jesus' love
and be God's instrument to save that soul for eternity.

Every day each of us is influencing others by
what we do or don't do, what we say or don't say.

When God chose him, Moses asked, "Who am I?"
The Lord promised to be with him and enable him.

Moses had to alter his plans and make sacrifices.
He devoted his abilities and assets to God's service.

The Lord calls us. Often we answer, "Who? Me?"
As we obey, He will be with us and enable us.

Each of us can say, "I'm only one. But I am one."
How extraordinary one ordinary person can be!

Be Tolerant

One garden book advises:
"If you want to enjoy watching butterflies,
put in plants that caterpillars like to eat."
But who wants to put up with those creatures!

It's hard to tolerate certain people, too.
A person who is not neat is difficult to live with.
Those who lack skill or pride in their work annoy us.
We are frustrated by people who are chronically late.
Their tardiness causes us to waste precious time.

Each person has the right to be herself or himself,
as long as this does not violate God's rules
or prevent others from being themselves.

Tolerance does not mean we condone sin.
It means we accept those who are different from us—
other styles, tastes, ideas, personalities.

All of us know we're not perfect.
But the good things we see in ourselves
help us tolerate our imperfections and quirks.
That's the way we need to love others, too.

We have to struggle to love some neighbors!
Love demands that we be tolerant.
Tolerance requires patience.

God doesn't zap us with patience and tolerance.
If we pray for these qualities, He develops them in us
by sending us difficult people to love.

How thankful we ought to be that our heavenly Father
loves us even though we are not yet butterflies!

Be Prepared

Many people live lives of quiet desperation.
God loves them intensely, but they don't know it yet.
Unless they trust in Jesus as Savior,
they'll spend eternity without hope.
It's up to us to tell them the Good News!

To make what we say about Jesus sound believable
our lives must be demonstrations of His influence.

Yet no matter how Christlike we try to act,
our lives are not so transparent that
God's love shines through perfectly.
We need words to communicate our faith clearly.

*"Always be prepared to give an answer
to everyone who asks you to give the reason
for the hope that you have. But do this
with gentleness and respect."* (1 Peter 3:15)

Jesus wants us to be witnesses, not judges or attorneys.
Our role is to confess, not to convert.

We ought to know what the Bible teaches about salvation.
We should be able to express what we believe.
Each of us can give a personal testimony:
>   What Jesus means to me.
>   How He affects my actions, my thinking, the way I feel.
>   How God has answered my prayers.

Sharing our faith helps strengthen and deepen it.
There is much joy in knowing God is using us
to make His kingdom come.

Win over Worry

To be human is to worry.
All of us at times are tormented by disturbing thoughts.
We do not always understand what is going on.
We fear some future event or possible happening.

Worry can move us into action.
If we discover a lump, anxiety can push us to see a doctor.
But most of the worrying we do serves no good purpose.
As we await biopsy results, worry only wears us down.

We allow a thin stream of fear to trickle through the mind.
One anxious thought leads to another, relentlessly
flooding our mind and washing away all other thoughts.
Worry drains us of energy and robs us of sleep.

It's very difficult to have an empty mind,
not to think about anything at all.
To get rid of anxious thoughts we must fill our mind
with positive, reinforcing ideas that build up courage.

Jesus assures us our heavenly Father knows what we need.
"Do not worry about tomorrow . . . " (Matthew 6:34)
Paul writes, *"The Lord is near. Do not be anxious
about anything. . . . "* (Philippians 4:5-6)

We do not know what God is going to do next.
We do know God loves us. He is always with us and
works for the good of those who love Him.
God will provide. He will give us strength.

When worrisome thoughts seep into our minds,
let's remind ourselves again and again of God's truths.
Peace of mind will be ours as we trust in the Lord.
He is able to do far more than we dare ask or dream.

Declaration of Dependence

I am not independent.
To keep life running smoothly and safely
I depend on a variety of people to supply
water, food, clothing, fuel, health care
and a multitude of services I often take for granted.

I depend also on things for comfort and efficiency.
The love of money is the root of all evil,
but a steady income can solve a lot of problems.
How blessed I am to have a roof over my head,
a cozy bed, a reliable car and dependable appliances!

Jesus reminds me:
*"A man's life does not consist in the
abundance of his possessions.
Do not set your heart on what you will
eat or drink; do not worry about it. . . .
your Father knows that you need them."*
(Luke 12:15, 29-30)

Ultimately my dependence is not on people or things.
It is on God.
I thank and praise Him for everything I have.
I trust Him for my future.

My heavenly Father is in control.
He was in control of the world before I was born.
He will be in control long after I'm gone.
He knows my needs. He loves me dearly.
He may not give me everything I want or expect.
But He will provide in the best possible way,
giving me whatever is for my eternal good.

Children of God

"Who in the world do you think you are?"
When people ask that, it's usually a put-down.
They intend to put us in our place.

Our heavenly Father reminds us
we are His children. That elevates us!
He intends to put us in His place—heaven!

*"How great is the love the Father has lavished
on us, that we should be called children of God!
And that is what we are!"* (1 John 3:1)

How do we rate such a noble position?
We don't. It's pure grace!
God's undeserved love!

Incredible as it may seem,
the Son of God came down to where we are
to enable us to rise to where He is!

Jesus was totally forsaken by His Father
that we might never be forsaken by Him.
How much He loves us!

Our Lord was put to death for us
that we might live eternally for Him.
We who believe in Christ are alive in Him.

Jesus lives in us, is united with us.
We can be filled with the fullness of God.
We can be more and more like Him.

Loving Touch

A phone company urges: reach out and touch someone.
But our phone call may be greeted by an answering machine.
We even receive calls from electronic devices!
Automated teller machines take care of banking needs.
We buy gasoline at self-service islands.
In our high-tech society we are often out of touch.

We've long known that babies need to be touched.
To develop full potential they need tender loving care.
We never outgrow that need.

Many people have no tender physical contact with anyone.
Those rarely touched have lower self-esteem.

Our Lord commands us: love one another.
Physical contact can transmit deep-felt emotion.
We deliver our message in a direct and caring way.
The reality of human touch makes God's love tangible.

We can encourage the disheartened by a pat on the back.
A gentle rub on someone's shoulder is reassuring.
To support another's arm with ours gives confidence.
A stroke on cheek or brow refreshes.
Holding someone's hand makes him or her more secure.
A hug lets a person know we really care.
Hugs make living easier and more worthwhile.

When someone is hurting and we don't know what to say,
just being there with a gentle touch clearly tells,
"I want to share your trouble, to make it my own.
You may depend on me to do whatever I can."

God put "skin hunger" in all of us.
We need to touch and to be touched.

What the World Needs Now

Dear Lord,
I work in a dog-eat-dog world.
Some who get to the top knock other people down,
walk all over them or kick them out of the way.

You tell me, *"Whoever wants to become great among
you must be your servant."* (Mark 10:43)
Your philosophy sounds great when I'm in church,
but it's hard to practice in the workplace.

You say if I humble myself, I'll be exalted.
I'd never have a chance for promotion if I act that way!

Jesus, I know You love me. I believe You are all-wise.
You wouldn't tell me to do what is foolish, impractical.
I must be governed by what You say—not what others do.
I want to do what I ought, but alone I can't.
It's going to be a tough struggle. I need Your strength.

When those around me lie, cheat, steal,
help me be honest—always aware of Your presence.
While coworkers goof off and do as little as possible,
may I work with all my heart, as working for You.

If they criticize and resent me when I do that,
enable me to be dependable, conscientious.

Though my boss shows me no respect or appreciation,
keep me mindful that I am Your representative.

When others act and speak as if You are not real,
give me courage to demonstrate my faith in You.

Some I work with are unloving and unlovable.
Have mercy on them.
They may not be loved at home or anywhere else.
You love them. Help me show them love.

Move On

We live in a chaotic and neurotic world.
Even those who love and serve the Lord
at times are discouraged and confused.
Traumatic experiences happen to us;
situations seem impossible; the future, bleak.

God's ancient people had troubles, too.
After escaping their Egyptian slavemasters,
they came to a dead end. They were terrified.
The enemy was behind them. The Red Sea before them.
Moses told them, *"Do not be afraid . . . you will see
the deliverance the Lord will bring you."* (Exodus 14:13)
Then the Lord said, "Move on!"

God did not transport them painlessly
to the Promised Land. The journey was tough.
He provided for them in miraculous ways,
but they had to learn to trust and obey.
God went before them; they had to follow
moving on one step at a time.

Though our situation may seem hopeless,
we have the assurance: God is with us.
We are His people. We must trust and obey.

Fearlessly we can be firm and move on!
With God's help we can cope with our problems
and handle any obstacle that lies in our path.
He goes before us opening the necessary doors.
Our Father makes the impossible possible!

Deeds Demonstrate Love

Special company for dinner!
Martha rushed around getting things ready.
No wonder she was disgusted to see her sister Mary
just sitting at Jesus' feet listening to what He said.
That didn't seem fair. Martha blamed Jesus,
"Don't You care that I'm left doing all the work?"

How shocked Martha was when Jesus praised Mary,
saying she had chosen the one thing needed.

God wants us to spend time listening to Him.
We are to take time to worship Him,
praising Him for His majesty and mercy.
We need to study His Word, to meditate on it.
That's how we grow and get better acquainted with Him.
We draw strength, meeting with our Lord on a regular basis.

Yet when Jesus describes the Judgment scene,
He does not commend the faithful for their piety,
Bible knowledge or attendance at worship services.

"I was hungry and you gave me something to eat,
I was thirsty and you gave me something to drink,
I was a stranger and you invited me in,
I needed clothes and you clothed me,
I was sick and you looked after me,
I was in prison and you came to visit me."
(Matthew 25:35-36)

God showers bounteous, undeserved love upon us.
We respond to His love with love.
Such love impels us to listen in wonder at His feet,
then moves us to action.
In ordinary, undramatic deeds of kindness we say,
"God loves you. That's why I do.
I love Him dearly. I'm loving Him by loving you."

We Can Change

"Confession is good for the soul."
That's not necessarily so.

After he had betrayed Jesus for thirty silver coins,
Judas was filled with remorse and returned the money.
He confessed, "I have sinned."
It didn't do any good. He didn't go far enough.

Our Lord died a terrible death because of Judas' sin.
Jesus forgave those who killed Him.
Surely He included Judas.
But Judas didn't request or receive God's forgiveness.

Sometimes we make a similar mistake.
We concentrate on our sin problem.
We should also concentrate on God's solution.

We often fail to do what we ought.
We do the very things our heavenly Father forbids.
Awareness of this problem is only the first step.
Regrets and remorse do not lighten the load of guilt.

We need to come to our loving Lord,
confessing our faults.
We must surrender them, lay them on Jesus.

When we turn over our sins to Jesus, He removes them.
When we turn over our lives to Him, He remodels them.

Change Me!

Dear Lord,
I do not understand how much You love me.
I'm glad Your love isn't limited by the size of my mind.
Help me believe what I cannot conceive.
May I never forget You love me,
even though I am not loveworthy.

Forgive me for grieving You,
for failing to love You, myself and others,
for disappointing and disgusting You.

In spite of myself You love me!
Through Jesus You've drawn me to Yourself.
You've made me one with You!
Me! United with the Ruler of the universe!
Me! Reconciled to the Holy One!

You sacrificed Jesus to make this possible.
Your only Son died for me! Incredible!

Now He lives in me, and I in Him.
I cling to the hope You give me.
"If anyone is in Christ, he is a new creation;
the old has gone, the new has come!" (2 Corinthians 5:17)

Change me, Lord. Renew me.
Enable me to become what You want me to be.

The Tie that Binds

God binds us to Himself in love.
The most astounding, comforting fact is: God loves us.
He loved us enough to give His very best.
God sacrificed His only Son that, believing in Him,
we might become forgiven children of God.

Each of us can say:
God loves me personally. Jesus died for me!
Because God loves me, I love Him.
My love for Him is often very feeble and fragile.
Yet God loves me "in spite of" rather than "because of."

Since the Lord loves me unconditionally, I can love myself.
He gives me a sense of security, of self-worth.
I want to become all He desires me to be.

Because God loves me, I am free to love others.
He loves everyone. I am to love everyone, too.
My life ought to be a mirror reflecting His love,
treating everybody as a worthwhile human being,
someone deeply loved by our heavenly Father.
Impossible! Only God in me can do that.
He loves those around me through me.

God's love poured into other lives overflows
into my life. I am blessed by Him through them.
Love binds us to God and to one another.

Love is God's idea.
It's the mightiest force in the world.

A Plan for My Life

God has a plan for me.
He and I together
will see it come to pass.

At times obstacles and setbacks
discourage and weary me.
I'm tempted to give up.

But I trudge onward
knowing God is with me
ready to provide all my needs.

I want to fulfill His purpose.
He will give me the strength I need
to keep me going.

Today's the Day

Each new sunrise
is a fresh opportunity.
God is saying, "Here is another chance."

Life exists only
in the now—right now.
Only today is ours. It's all we really have.

Yesterday is a memory
to be cherished or abandoned.
We learn from its experience, then let it go.

We ought not
live as though there will
be no tomorrow. We must plan and dream.

But we had better
live as though there
is only today lest it slip away unused.

Whatever good
we can do, we must not neglect
or postpone. The days of love are short.

One Day at a Time

This is the day the Lord has made;
I will rejoice and be glad in it. *
There might not be much to laugh about.
Tears may flow, and
pain torment my body or mind.
Frustration and weariness
may slow me down.
But I will rejoice and be glad.
"The Lord is with me;
I will not be afraid." *
Nothing will happen to me today
that the Lord and I can't handle.

I can do it.
I can take it.
I will make it!
"I will not die but live." *
One day at a time.

"The Lord is with me;
He is my helper." *
He will give me wisdom to make decisions,
strength to bear my burdens,
courage to face whatever comes my way.

I will *"give thanks to the Lord, for he is good;*
his love endures forever." *

*Assurances from Psalm 118
(24, 6, 17a, 7a, 29)

*"Keep yourselves
in God's love. . ."*
(Jude 21)